THE CIVIL RIGHTS MOVEMENT

BY JIM OLLHOFF

Published by ABDO Publishing Company, 8000 West 78th Street, Suite 310, Edina, MN 55439. Copyright ©2011 by Abdo Consulting Group, Inc. International copyrights reserved in all countries. No part of this book may be reproduced in any form without written permission from the publisher. ABDO & Daughters™ is a trademark and logo of ABDO Publishing Company.

Printed in the United States of America, North Mankato, Minnesota.
112010
012011

♻ PRINTED ON RECYCLED PAPER

Editor: John Hamilton
Graphic Design: John Hamilton
Cover Design: Neil Klinepier
Cover Photo: Getty Images
Interior Photos and Illustrations: Corbis-pgs 10-11, 12, 23; Getty Images-pgs 12, 13, 15, 19, 22, 24, 25, 26-27, 27, 28-28; Granger Collection-pgs 4-5, 8, 9, 14, 16-17, 18, 20-21; iStockphoto-pgs 6-7.

Library of Congress Cataloging-in-Publication Data

Ollhoff, Jim, 1959-
  The civil rights movement / Jim Ollhoff.
    p. cm. -- (African-American history)
  Includes index.
  ISBN 978-1-61714-709-8
  1. Civil rights movements--United States--History--20th century--Juvenile literature. 2. African Americans--Civil rights--History--20th century--Juvenile literature. 3. United States--Race relations--Juvenile literature. I. Title.
  E185.61.O37 2011
  323.0973--dc22
                              2010038246

CONTENTS

THE CIVIL RIGHTS MOVEMENT

Racism is like a brick wall made of hatred, fear, and ignorance. From 1954 to 1964, that wall started to come down, little by little, brick by brick. During this decade, the civil rights movement saw a racist and unjust society begin to make real progress. It took the courage of brilliant black leaders. It took court cases and federal action. It took nonviolent resistance. And, tragically, it took the blood of innocent people, killed for seeking freedom and equality.

There has always been racism. Unfortunately, there probably always will be. There will probably always be people who are full of hatred for one group or another. However, the civil rights movement was a time when the ugliness of great injustice was revealed for everyone to see. Before the civil rights movement, injustices and inequality were tolerated in the United States.

There is still racism today, and equality is still only a dream for many. But the courage of the leaders of the civil rights movement brought a new freedom for African Americans.

Martin Luther King Jr. leads a protest march from Selma, Alabama, to the state capital of Montgomery in March 1965. The protesters were demanding voter registration rights for African Americans.

Martin Luther King Jr.

SEGREGATION IN THE SCHOOLS

Since the late 1800s, state courts had ruled that schools could be segregated. In other words, they said it was okay to have "whites-only" schools and "blacks-only" schools. However, in the 1930s and in the years following, many people challenged that belief.

In 1954, the United States Supreme Court heard a series of cases questioning segregation laws. Thurgood Marshall argued the case for the black community. He said that separate schools meant that the schools were unequal, and did not give black children a fair education. The Supreme Court agreed, and struck down segregation in schools in the case of *Brown v. Board of Education*.

Elizabeth Eckford *(in sunglasses) is verbally abused as she walks to class in September 1957 at Little Rock Central High School, in Little Rock, Arkansas.*

Some communities ignored the Supreme Court's ruling. Others partially ignored it. Little Rock, Arkansas, became a famous battleground. In September 1957, a number of black students tried to enroll at an all-white high school. White segregationists opposed the black enrollment. Tempers and lawsuits increased. Finally, segregationist Governor Orval Faubus sent in Arkansas National Guard soldiers to keep the peace and turn away the African American students.

By the end of September 1957, President Dwight Eisenhower, angered by the governor's disobedience of the Supreme Court ruling, sent in federal troops to enforce integration and protect the black students.

In 1967, Thurgood Marshall became the first African American to serve on the United States Supreme Court.

Justice Thurgood Marshall, in front of the United States Supreme Court building in Washington, DC.

Thurgood Marshall (1908–1993)

Thurgood Marshall was the great-grandson of a slave. He applied to law school at the University of Maryland, but couldn't attend because he was black. He went to another law school, became a lawyer, and sued the University of Maryland for its segregation policies. He became the chief counsel for the National Association for the Advancement of Colored People (NAACP). He is best known for arguing at the Supreme Court for integration, in a series of cases called *Brown v. Board of Education*. He argued that separate schools meant that schools were unequal.

In 1967, Marshall became the first African American to serve on the United States Supreme Court.

A MURDER
THAT ROCKED
THE NATION

The civil rights movement had many leaders and many events that gave it energy and drive. One of the most tragic events was the murder of a 14-year-old boy named Emmett Till. The horrifying event gave racial injustice a human face, and pushed more people across the nation to demand civil rights.

Emmett Till was an African American boy visiting family members in rural Mississippi in 1955. While at a grocery store with some friends to buy candy, he supposedly flirted or whistled at a white woman. He was later kidnapped at gunpoint. His body was found several days later. He had been badly beaten, tortured, and shot.

Till's mother insisted on a public funeral with an open casket, so that everyone could see what had been done to her child. An estimated 50,000 people came to the funeral and saw his body. The pictures of his beaten body were in newspapers across the country. The horror of the murder enraged the nation.

A view of the 1955 trial in Sumner, Mississippi, of Roy Bryant and J.W. Milam, accused of murdering 14-year-old Emmett Till.

Above: *A photo of Emmett Till on the plaque that marks his grave in Alsip, Illinois.*
Left: *Emmett Till's grief-stricken mother, Mamie Bradley, as her son is laid to rest.*

Two local men, Roy Bryant and J. W. Milam, were arrested for the kidnapping and murder of Emmett Till. They were put on trial, and a jury of 12 white men found them not guilty.

After the trial, the two men sold their story to a national magazine, describing how they beat and killed Emmett Till. The Fifth Amendment of the Constitution of the United States forbids people from being tried twice for the same crime. So, the two men couldn't be put on trial again. People wondered if they were telling the truth or not, or whether more people were involved in the crime.

The murder of Emmet Till enraged both blacks and whites, causing many people to join the civil rights movement.

Malcolm X was an activist and public speaker. He was one of the most influential advocates for African American rights during the civil rights movement.

Malcolm X (1925–1965)

Born with the name Malcolm Little, Malcolm X became one of the most influential black Americans during the civil rights movement. While he was in prison in the 1950s, he joined a religious group called the Nation of Islam. He became their spokesperson. He began his career as a civil rights activist by proclaiming black pride. A powerful speaker, he believed that white people were inferior to blacks, and that white people were a race of devils. Many people were alarmed by his violent tone.

After several experiences, Malcolm X left the Nation of Islam and began to tone down his violent language. Instead, he discussed peaceful approaches to equality. He was assassinated in 1965 by members of the Nation of Islam. He was killed just as he began to embrace peace, understanding, and nonviolence.

THE RISE OF MARTIN LUTHER KING JR.

One of the greatest leaders to come out of any historical movement was Reverend Martin Luther King Jr.

A great visionary, his ideas continue to be an inspiration for people of all skin colors. King combined his beliefs in God with his views on civil rights. He said that blacks needed to stand up for their rights, but they had to do it peacefully and nonviolently.

King invited white people to stand with black people side-by-side in the struggle for equality. He said that people should never stoop to the level of hatred shown by the racists. He said the civil rights movement could be won with love and peace.

Martin Luther King Jr. at the March on Washington, August 28, 1963.

Martin Luther King Jr. was born in Atlanta, Georgia, in 1929. He wanted to become a pastor, so he studied in Pennsylvania and Boston, Massachusetts. He became pastor of Dexter Avenue Baptist Church in Montgomery, Alabama. Once there, he became active in the civil rights movement.

In 1957, King and others created an organization called the Southern Christian Leadership Conference (SCLC). The SCLC helped organize many of the civil rights movement's activities. The organization decided to try to engage people in mass nonviolent action when injustice was being done. The SCLC also vowed to be open to all people, regardless of religion, background, or skin color.

THE BUS TO CIVIL RIGHTS

Another event that rocked the nation began as a very simple act. In December 1955, city buses in Montgomery, Alabama, were segregated. White people sat in the front part of the bus, and black people were required to sit in the back of the bus. The law forbade a black person from sitting in the same seat as a white person. One day, a white man got on a bus that was full of people. The bus driver told some black people in one of the seats to move so that the white man could sit down. A woman named Rosa Parks did not move. She was then arrested.

The black community decided to boycott the Montgomery buses for a day in protest of Rosa Parks's arrest. They asked the pastors in Montgomery—including Martin Luther King Jr.—to tell their congregations to boycott the buses. The boycott was so successful that they decided to continue with it.

Rosa Parks

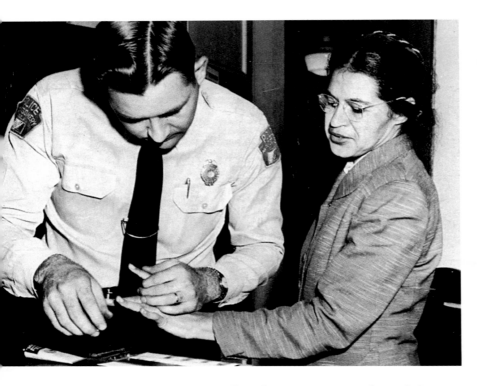

Rosa Parks *is fingerprinted by a Montgomery, Alabama, police officer on February 22, 1956, following her arrest for her role in organizing a boycott of the city's buses to protest their racial segregation of passengers.*

The bus company refused to change its segregation policies, even though the company was losing a lot of money because of fewer riders. Blacks were using taxicabs instead of buses. So, whites increased the price of cabs, hoping to force black customers back to the buses. Instead, the black community created an independent taxi service.

City leaders continued to push to end the boycott while keeping segregationist policies. Finally, Martin Luther King Jr. was arrested and tried for conspiracy. He was found guilty at his first trial, but he appealed the decision to a higher court and his sentence was suspended.

By this time, the Montgomery bus boycott was national news, and people from all over the country pledged their support to the boycotters. Finally, the legal challenge to bus segregation ended. In December 1956, a year after Rosa Parks refused to give up her seat, the courts said that bus segregation was unconstitutional.

*Martin Luther King Jr. at the end of the
Montgomery bus boycott, Montgomery,
Alabama, December 26, 1956.*

NONVIOLENT PROTESTS

Tackling injustice on buses was just the beginning for the civil rights movement. Other protests soon followed. In many Southern states, inequality was made into law. Many areas had segregated restaurants, parks, and public facilities. These laws were sometimes called "Jim Crow laws."

In 1960, four black college students went to a "whites only" lunch counter at a diner. They were refused service, but they stayed in the diner anyway. Other college students, both black and white, joined them. Students took up space in "whites only" restaurants, hurting the businesses that refused to serve them. These protests became known as "sit-ins" and they became a popular and effective way to promote change.

Four young black men sitting at a segregated lunch counter in a drug store in Jackson, Mississippi, soon to be arrested by police officers for refusing an order to leave, July 13, 1961.

Freedom rider David Dennis *sits aboard a bus, where he and others are escorted by two armed National Guardsmen on the way from Montgomery, Alabama, to Jackson, Mississippi, in early 1961.*

Over time, the Jim Crow laws began to change, and segregated "whites only" areas began to disappear. However, sometimes racist attitudes remained. College students and others began taking bus trips throughout the Southern states to test the new desegregation laws. They stopped at places and tried to use facilities that were formerly marked as "whites only." Sometimes, these "freedom riders" were attacked by angry white mobs.

In June 1963, a young girl at the funeral of Medgar Evers holds a program with a photo of the slain civil rights activist.

Medgar Evers (1925–1963)

Medgar Evers was born in Decatur, Mississippi. During World War II, he fought in Europe for freedom. After the war, he realized he had to fight for freedom in his own home state. He became president of the Regional Council of Negro Leadership, which fought for civil rights. He applied to the University of Mississippi Law School, which was segregated at the time. His application was rejected. He sued the school, and the court ruled that segregation was against the United States Constitution.

In 1954, Medgar Evers took an important position in the NAACP. However, tragedy struck in 1963 when he was murdered in the driveway of his own home. Byron De La Beckwith, a Ku Klux Klan member, was arrested and tried. The trial resulted in a hung jury, which means the jury could not come to a decision. A second trial also resulted in a hung jury. Finally, in 1993, a jury convicted De La Beckwith of murdering Evers, and he was sentenced to life in prison.

Songs were written in the 1960s about Medgar Evers. His death became another rallying point in the civil rights movement. The 1996 movie *Ghosts of Mississippi* tells the story of the Medgar Evers trial.

BIRMINGHAM, ALABAMA

In April 1963, there were widespread protests against segregation in Birmingham, Alabama. Martin Luther King Jr., one of the leaders of the movement, was arrested and jailed. He was told by a number of white pastors that justice could be won in the courts, and that protests in the streets were unnecessary. In response, King wrote the famous *Letter from Birmingham Jail.* In it, he said without nonviolent direct action, true justice could never be won. He said it was not only helpful to disobey unjust segregation laws, but that people had a duty to disobey those laws. He said, "Injustice anywhere is a threat to justice everywhere."

Police officers try to lift a fallen demonstrator off the ground on May 6, 1963, in Birmingham, Alabama. She was arrested for "failure to move on" when warned by the police.

African American children are attacked by dogs and high-pressure water hoses during the May 1963 Birmingham, Alabama, protest against racial segregation.

Then, in May 1963, there was a peaceful march of black Americans in Birmingham. Commissioner of Public Safety Bull Conner tried to stop the march. He used fire hoses, clubs, and police dogs against the peaceful marchers. This was a defining moment in the civil rights movement because of television. Bull Conner's brutal tactics were broadcast on news channels nationwide. People across the United States watched the stark images of hatred and violence of the segregationists. People, both white and black, once again saw segregation for what it was: injustice that came from hatred and ignorance.

THE MARCH ON WASHINGTON

On August 28, 1963, there was a massive protest in Washington, DC. More than 250,000 people came to the Lincoln Memorial to protest racial injustice. City authorities feared that the crowd would become hostile. But then Martin Luther King Jr. spoke.

King's speech is sometimes called the "I Have a Dream" speech. He didn't tell people how they had been wronged, hurt, or victimized. Instead, he gave people a positive vision of the future, where people of all skin colors could live in peace and harmony.

For his work to end racial discrimination, in 1964 King became the youngest person to win a Nobel Peace Prize.

"I have a dream that one day this nation will rise up and live out the true meaning of its creed: 'We hold these truths to be self-evident, that all men are created equal.' I have a dream that one day…the sons of former slaves and the sons of former slave owners will be able to sit down together at the table of brotherhood….I have a dream that my four little children will one day live in a nation where they will not be judged by the color of their skin but by the content of their character."
—Martin Luther King Jr.

BREAKING DOWN THE
WALLS OF RACISM

In the 1950s and 1960s, racist attitudes were widespread. Many unjust laws were still enforced. Breaking down injustice and racism was a journey that took many steps. It took great leaders, like Martin Luther King Jr. It took tragic crimes, like the murder of Medgar Evers. It took people who were willing to challenge injustice, like Rosa Parks.

The walls of segregation and racism started to crumble in the 1950s and 1960s because of brave people who were willing to take risks for civil rights. The walls came down because of thousands of courageous acts by people demanding freedom and dignity.

The Jim Crow laws came down also because of government actions. The courts ruled that racist laws were unconstitutional. Presidents said that racial injustice had to stop. Congress passed laws that prevented injustice.

There will probably always be ignorance, hatred, and racism. But our society is better today because of the courageous acts of individuals in the civil rights movement.

Martin Luther King Jr. leading the March on Washington, August 28, 1963, in Washington, DC.

GLOSSARY

BOYCOTT

To refuse to buy from a company, or use its services. Boycotts are often a form of protest or punishment.

CIVIL RIGHTS

The rights of all individuals to participate equally in their communities.

DESEGREGATION

Integrating black people and white people into the same facility, school, or place of business. After desegregation laws were passed, there could no longer be "whites only" facilities. Desegregation ended the forced separation of blacks and whites.

JIM CROW LAWS

Laws that enforced the separation of black people and white people. Public facilities in the South, for example, often had signs offering facilities for "whites only" and signs offering facilities for "colored." The phrase "Jim Crow" may have its origins in a song-and-dance routine called "Jump Jim Crow." The song first appeared in the late 1820s, and featured a white actor who played an African American while in blackface makeup. The song mocked African Americans, and heightened racial stereotypes.

KU KLUX KLAN

Often referred to as the KKK, the Ku Klux Klan is an extreme, racist organization that believes in the supremacy of white people over all others.

It was formed in the Southern states after the Civil War. The group used violence to oppose equal rights for African Americans. Ku Klux Klan members often disguised themselves by dressing in white robes with hoods, and burned wooden crosses as a Klan symbol. The Ku Klux Klan still exists today, with independent chapters across the country, with most in the Southern United States.

Nobel Prize

An international prize that is awarded each year in chemistry, physics, physiology, economics, medicine, and the promotion of peace.

Racism

The belief that people of one skin color are better than a people of another skin color; or, that individuals of a certain skin color have certain characteristics *because* of their skin color.

Segregation

The practice of separating blacks and whites. A segregated school, for example, could only have either white children or black children.

Sit-in

A common and effective way to challenge segregationist businesses. For example, people would often sit at segregated restaurants without ordering. This hurt the business of the restaurant, and often forced the business to desegregate.

Unconstitutional

A law that the court system decides violates the rules and procedures of the United States Constitution. Segregation laws designed to separate white and blacks were ruled unconstitutional, and therefore illegal.

INDEX